Greater Than a To Ljubljana Slovenia

50 Travel Tips from a Local

Andreja Dintinjana

Copyright © 2017 CZYK Publishing
All Rights Reserved. No part of this publication may be reproduced, including scanning and photocopying, or distributed in any form or by any means, electronic or mechanical, or stored in a database or retrieval system without prior written permission from the publisher.

Disclaimer: The publisher has put forth an effort in preparing and arranging this book. The information provided herein by the author is provided "as is". Use this information at your own risk. Consult your doctor before engaging in any medical activities. The publisher and author disclaim any liabilities for any loss of profit or commercial or personal damages resulting from the information contained in this book.

Order Information: To order this title please email lbrenenc@gmail.com or visit GreaterThanATourist.com. A bulk discount can be provided.

Cover Template Creator: Lisa Rusczyk Ed. D. using Canva.
Cover Creator: Lisa Rusczyk Ed. D.
Image: https://pixabay.com/en/ljubljana-river-slovenia-bridge-2149704/

Lock Haven, PA
All rights reserved.
ISBN: 9781549800719

>TOURIST

Andreja Dintinjana

BOOK DESCRIPTION

Are you excited about planning your next trip?

Do you want to try something new?

Would you like some guidance from a local?

If you answered yes to any of these questions, then this Greater Than a Tourist book is for you.

Greater Than a Tourist Ljubljana Slovenia by Andreja Dintinjana offers the inside scoop on Ljubljana. Most travel books tell you how to sightsee. Although there's nothing wrong with that, as a part of the Greater than a Tourist series, this book will give you tips from someone who lives at your next travel destination. In these pages, you'll discover local advice that will help you throughout your trip. Travel like a local. Slow down and get to know the people and the culture of a place. By the time you finish this book, you will be eager and prepared to travel to your next destination.

Andreja Dintinjana

>TOURIST

TABLE OF CONTENTS

BOOK DESCRIPTION

TABLE OF CONTENTS

DEDICATION

ABOUT THE AUTHOR

HOW TO USE THIS BOOK

FROM THE PUBLISHER

WELCOME TO > TOURIST

INTRODUCTION

1. Get To Know Slovenia

2. Slovenian Language

3. Get To Know Ljubljana

4. Brief History Of Ljubljana

5. Ljubljana City Center

6. Ljubljana Squares

7. Ljubljana Streets

8. Ljubljana Bridges

9. Shopping In Ljubljana

10. Transportation In Ljubljana

11. Use A Bike To Move Around The City If You Want To Blend In Totally

12. Partying In Ljubljana

13. Visit The City Market In The Morning

14. Walk To The Ljubljana Castle, Locals Never Use The Funicular Railway

15. Lay Down, Relax And Feed The Squirrels In Park Tivoli

16. Visit Ljubljana ZOO

17. Have A Morning Jog Around Koseze Pond

18. Cycle Your Way Around Ljubljana On POT

19. Read A Book On The City "Beach", But Don't Swim!

20. Craving Something Sweet?

21. Take A Walk In The Botanical Garden Of Ljubljana

22. Have A Unique Friday Night Experience On Metelkova – Heart Of Ljubljana's Alternative Culture

23. Climb Your Way Out Of Foggy Ljubljana

24. Swim In Slovenia's Deepest Lake

25. Enjoy A Coffee With A View

26. Have A Beer In The Union Brewery

>TOURIST

27. Listen To A Summer Concert In Križanke

28. Looking For A Swimming Pool?

29. Try Traditional Balkan Food

30. SUP Your Way Through The City

31. Cool Down On A Hot Summer Day In Iška Gorge

32. Have A Walk Through The Village In The Middle Of Ljubljana

33. Visit The Famous Cemetery

34. Explore The Village Of Bistra

35. Try The Traditional Slovenian Cuisine

36. When The Locals Dine Out

37. Friday Lunch At Open Kitchen

38. Coffee Culture

39. Try To Find Something Useful On The Flea Market

40. Take A One Day Trip

41. Visit A Cave

42. Bled Or Bohinj?

43. Hiking

44. To The Coast

45. Go Wine Tasting

46. Soča Adrenaline Sports

47. Have A Relaxing Day In The Spa

48. Bear Safari

49. Visit The Big Pasture Plateau

50. Souvenir Ideas

Top Reasons to Book This Trip

Our Story

Notes

DEDICATION

This book is dedicated to J. B. D., hoping one day you are able to experience all of this yourself.

Andreja Dintinjana

ABOUT THE AUTHOR

Andreja is a Geography student, living and studying in Ljubljana for six years now. Originally from the coastal town of Koper, she, as many others, didn't like Ljubljana before she moved there. She taught of it as a fogy and dirty capital with way too much traffic. This is how she remembered Ljubljana from occasional visits to her grandma more than 10 years ago. After moving here, she realized that both, her and the city too, have changed. Today she is proud to live in one of the nicest places in Europe.

Andreja Dintinjana

HOW TO USE THIS BOOK

The Greater Than a Tourist book series was written by someone who has lived in an area for over three months. The goal of this book is to help travelers either dream or experience different locations by providing opinions from a local. The author has made suggestions based on their own experiences. Please do your own research before traveling to the area in case the suggested places are unavailable.

Andreja Dintinjana

FROM THE PUBLISHER

Traveling can be one of the most important parts of a person's life. The anticipation and memories that you have are some of the best. As a publisher of the Greater Than a Tourist book series, as well as the popular 50 Things to Know book series, we strive to help you learn about new places, spark your imagination, and inspire you. Wherever you are and whatever you do I wish you safe, fun, and inspiring travel.

Lisa Rusczyk Ed. D.
CZYK Publishing

Andreja Dintinjana

>TOURIST

WELCOME TO > TOURIST

Andreja Dintinjana

INTRODUCTION

You will love Ljubljana. Either for the kindness of its people, for the delicious mix of tastes the Slovenian cuisine offers, for the many green spaces that help the city breathe or for its manageable size, which makes it easy to explore it. I am sure after a few days, Ljubljana will feel like home to you. It has that kind of homey atmosphere.

Before you start exploring the city, it is very important you get yourself a good city map. You can get one in a tourist information center or in any hotel and hostel located in the city. This book doesn't have much sense if you don't know where the places are located. Secondly, you can never see and do everything the city has to offer. You don't need to cross all the streets, bridges and churches from your list. Experience the city slowly, with all your senses, instead of hurrying from one site to the other. Most importantly, relax and enjoy yourself because not every day you have a chance to be in the beautiful city of Ljubljana.

Andreja Dintinjana

1. Get To Know Slovenia

Slovenia is located in the southern part of Central Europe. Sometimes it is also classified as a part of Eastern or Southern Europe. The problems with the classification are the result of Slovenia's location on the crossroad of four main European regions; the Alps on the northwest, Pannonian Plain on the northeast, Dinarides on the south and the Mediterranean on the southwest.

Due to the position on the contact, Slovenia has a significant biological and geomorphological diversity, which is easily noticeable while traveling through the country, as you are able to see how fast the landscape changes. Slovenians are happy to praise about living in one of the most water-rich countries in Europe. Over 60 % of the territory is covered by forests.

The area of the country covers 20.000 square kilometers and has a population of 2 million. The biggest city is Ljubljana, followed by Maribor in the eastern part of the country. Other cities are significantly smaller. The human settlement of Slovenia is, in general, dispersed and uneven.

Historically, the territory of Slovenia has been part of many different state formations including the Roman Empire, the Habsburg Monarchy and the Socialist Federal Republic of Yugoslavia. In June 1991 Slovenia split from Yugoslavia and became an independent country. We entered NATO and the European Union in 2004 and became the first formerly communist country to join the Eurozone in 2007.

2. Slovenian Language

Historically Slovenia has been on the crossroad of Germanic, Romance, West Slavic, South Slavic and Hungarian culture and languages. The official language is Slovenian, which might sound similar to other Balkan languages, Russian, Polish, Slovak, Czech and a few other. However, it is not the same language as any of the stated. Most of the Slovenians understand Croatian, Bosnian and Serbian language due to the similarity and the fact, that during socialistic times the language classes were a part of school process. Other languages we do not understand. Even if we sound like Russians while cheering with the drinks, do not mistake it thinking the languages are almost the same. They are not. Also, please do not keep asking us about this all the time.

3. Get To Know Ljubljana

Ljubljana (pronounced lyoo-BLYAH-nah) is the capital and the largest city in Slovenia with around 280.000 inhabitants. It is a cultural, educational, economic, political and administrative center of Slovenia. The city center is located under the castle hill, on both sides of the River Ljubljanica. From the center, Ljubljana is expanding in every direction. As a consequence of the main transportation routes, shaped like a cross and connecting southwest part of the country with the northeastern and the northwestern part with the southeastern, the city has got a shape of a star, as the expansion is mostly taking place along the main roads.

The city of Ljubljana is situated in the Ljubljana Basin in Central Slovenia and has the elevation of around 300 meters. On the south, Ljubljana borders Ljubljana Marshes, 163 square kilometers big marsh with great biodiversity. On the north, the Ljubljana Basin borders the Alps. On a clear day, even from the city center you can enjoy the amazing view of the mountains.

4.Brief History Of Ljubljana

Ljubljana's first inhabitants were the pile-dwellers, who lived in a wood settlement on poles in the marshes south of Ljubljana. Ljubljana got its first name during the Roman times, when they called it Emona. It was located in the area where the navigable Ljubljanica came closest to the Castle Hill. The remains of the city walls have been renovated and today you are able to see a part of it near the city center. In the medieval times Ljubljana, under the Austrian rule, got the name Laibach. Later, in 1895, most of the city was destroyed by a huge earthquake, then followed a total makeover of the city image, which resulted in the city look you are able to experience today.

In 1945 Slovenia became part of the Socialist Federal Republic of Yugoslavia, which led to building lots of socialist neighborhoods, intended for socialist working class. Today those neighborhoods are mostly renovated, although you can still feel the spirit of the socialist times if you take a walk through some parts of Bežigrad,

Šiška, Fužine or Štepanjsko naselje.

In 1991 Ljubljana got its new role as a capital of the newly independent country. Before everyone got clear on what the actual vision of the city was, Slovenia joined the EU in 2004 which naturally meant Ljubljana had to have an EU-friendly vision for itself also. In 2016 Ljubljana got the European Green Capital title, which might mean we are headed in the right direction.

5. Ljubljana City Center

The center of Ljubljana is the place where all the tourist go. Even if you want to avoid the most typical tourist spots, you just cannot miss this one. And you shouldn't, as it is, although sometimes crowded, still one of Europe's best-kept secrets.

The architecture in the old city center is a mix of styles. While on the edge of Ljubljana you can find large buildings originating from the socialist era or later, the center still remains intact. The shape of the old part of the city dates back to the Middle Ages, when after the 1511 earthquake the city was rebuilt in Baroque style. After the 1895 earthquake demolished a big part of Ljubljana, it was rebuilt again, this time in Vienna Secession style. The major impact on the modern identity of the city had a famous Slovenian architect Jože Plečnik, who designed many of the features, including Triple Bridge, Slovene National and University Library and the Žale cemetery.

Andreja Dintinjana

Since 2007, the city center of Ljubljana is closed off for all motorized traffic. Once upon a time (15 years) all the traffic, including buses and trucks, was going across the Prešeren square and over the Triple Bridge. Try to imagine this while standing on the bridge today. Even the locals cannot imagine it anymore.

6. Ljubljana Squares

There is a fair number of squares in Ljubljana. The main one is Prešeren Square, located right next to the Triple Bridge in the old city center. It got named after the Slovenian poet France Prešeren, who is an author of the poem today used as our national anthem. His statue on the square is a popular meeting point.

The largest square in Ljubljana is the Republic Square, where in June 1991, the independence was declared. At its northern side stands The National Assembly Building. Congress Square is one of the main squares in the city center. Next to it there is Park Zvezda, a popular socializing spot. Here you can enjoy many open-air concerts and other events happening mostly during summer months. On the other side of River Ljubljanica, there is the Town Square, where the Town Hall is located. Other than these few well-known ones, Ljubljana also has many other interesting squares worth exploring.

7. Ljubljana Streets

The main street in the old part of the city is Čop Street, the traditional shopping street in the center, which connects Prešeren Square with the Slovene Street. Slovene Street was recently renovated, since then only the city buses and taxis are allowed to drive trough. The main post office is located on the corner of both. On Slovene Street there are many restaurants and bars. One of the main streets in the center is also Wolfova Street, connecting Park Zvezda with Prešeren Square.

Special title, in my opinion, goes to Trubarjeva Street, going from Prešeren Square to the east all up to the old Rog bike factory. It is a place with many interesting sites. There are cafes, bars, mini shops with all sorts of things, book shops and some hostels. The street is an interesting place to explore if you are attracted to alternative placcs with graffiti scribbled walls.

8. Ljubljana Bridges

Due to the River Ljubljanica, flowing through the center, there are many bridges to explore. Most of them are a piece of art itself. The most famous is the Triple Bridge, next to the Prešeren Square, which as it is obvious from its name, consists of three bridges, the bigger one and two smaller ones, one on each side of it.

If you wish to see where the dragon family is hanging out these days, visit the Dragon Bridge. Each of the dragons is resting on one of its corners. The bad thing is, there is a busy traffic road crossing the bridge. However, it looks as the dragons don't really mind. Between the Dragon Bridge and the Triple Bridge is located The Butchers Bridge. Do not let the name confuse you, you will not get butchered there. On the contrary, you might even get kissed because shortly after the opening, padlocks of couples in love started appearing on its steel wires, symbolizing declarations of eternal love.

On the other side of the Triple Bridge you can cross Ljubljanica over Šuštarski Bridge, where you often have a chance to enjoy street artists performances. Between the two, there is a small footbridge where the perfect shot of Prešeren Square and Triple Bridge can be shot.

9. Shopping In Ljubljana

The main and traditional shopping street in the center of Ljubljana is Čopova Street which connects Slovenska Street with Prešeren Square. There you mostly find the shops belonging to the well-known international chains. The shops offering the traditional Slovenian products are scattered around the city center. The biggest and most known complex of shopping malls in Ljubljana is BTC, located on the northeastern part of the city. It offers more than 500 shops and it is quite hard to navigate on foot as it covers the area of 250.000 square meters. It includes a main shopping mall called City Park, 16 smaller shopping malls, the biggest cinema center in the country Kolosej, the recently opened Plaza Hotel Ljubljana, a market, a mini-golf course, a waterpark with a spa center and an entertainment center with a casino, bowling, 3D cinema as well as two high-rise office buildings. One of these, the Crystal Palace, is with its 20 floors, the tallest building in Slovenia. If you are a shopping lover this just might be the place for you.

10. Transportation In Ljubljana

Ljubljana, as mentioned before, lays in the middle of Slovenian highway cross, meaning, it also represents one of the more important crossroads between Southern, Eastern and Central Europe. The main Slovenian airport (Jože Pučnik Airport) is located 20-30 minute drive north of Ljubljana.

Around the city there is a busy highway ring. Traveling by car, a good option is to park your car in one of the P+R (park and ride) parking lots as parking spaces in the city are limited. Don't forget to buy a vignette if you are entering the country on a highway.

The train station is located on the edge of the city center, right next to the main bus station. Although the train journey offers amazing views of the country's landscape, it can be devastatingly slow.

There is a quite effective city bus net, called LPP. All of the areas inside the city are covered by it as well as some of the locations in the vicinity of Ljubljana. To use it you need the Urbana card. You can get one in the tourist information centers, most city street kiosks and post offices for a one-time fee of €2. One journey costs €1.20, while you are free to change buses as many times as you wish in the time period of 90 minutes.

Your best option to move around the center is just to do what the locals do, meaning, walk or use a bicycle.

Andreja Dintinjana

>TOURIST

"The world is a book, and those who do not travel read only a page."

— Saint Augustine

Andreja Dintinjana

11. Use A Bike To Move Around The City If You Want To Blend In Totally

There are more than enough reasons locals choose to move from one part of the city to another by a bicycle. Firstly, there is a traffic jam issue. Everyone travels to work and back home at approximately the same time, which results in some traffic jams inside the city and even more on the highway circle around Ljubljana. Often a bicycle is the fastest way to travel around the city. Secondly, if you own a car, there is always a problem with parking spaces. Cyclists have no problem parking their bike next to any pole like structure.

Besides being convenient, city cycling presents some kind of a tradition in Ljubljana. Around the city, you can see plenty of elderly people returning from a market on their old bikes with a basket full of groceries. They have probably been doing that for many years. However, not only elderly people have old bikes. Sometimes on the streets, it seems as if a contest is going on of 'who has the oldest bike'. In the socialist times, there was a famous bicycle factory in the center of Ljubljana, the Rog factory. It is still very common for people to use those famous bikes that have probably been repaired countless times.

If you are planning to stay in Ljubljana for a longer period, you can try buying a bicycle. Best way to do that is on a website Bolha that is something like Slovenian eBay. On the other hand, you can just ask around as often there are auctions of old bikes happening. The price goes from €20 to €150 for a second (or third) hand bike. Do not forget to buy a very good locker and always lock your bike, as bike theft is common in otherwise exceptionally safe city of Ljubljana. If your stay will only be for a short period of time, consider using the city bikes Bicike-lj.

12. Partying In Ljubljana

Considering the small size of the city, Ljubljana's party scene is not bad. The credit probably goes to many students studying (and partying) in Ljubljana between the months of October and June. The tourist take their places during the summer months. Meaning, you can party in Ljubljana all year round.

For the locals, partying usually starts with some drinks in one of the pubs next to River Ljubljanica. When the outside sections of the pubs and bars get closed after midnight, people usually move into one of the clubs. There is no "party street" in Ljubljana, where most of the clubs would be lined up, like in many other cities. The places that offer a good party vibe are mostly scattered close to the city center and around. It is a good idea to check what events are going on in different clubs on a particular day. A club you liked yesterday might have a totally different scene today. You can join an organized Ljubljana Pub Crawl where you will definitely have an unforgettable experience.

13. Visit The City Market In The Morning

Ljubljana city market is one of the rare places you can actually buy locally produced food. Most of the sellers come from the outskirts of Ljubljana and offer good quality food. Outdoor there is a section with fruits and vegetables where you can buy seasonal goods. Right next to it there are sections with flowers and clothes. The market also has an indoor section with different types of meat, fish, cheese, bread and other types of food.

If you have a chance to cook, a good idea is to buy some food on the market and try to follow a Slovenian recipe, as restaurants in the center of the city can sometimes be quite expensive. Depends on your budget and the amount of time you are going to spend in Ljubljana of course.

If you decide to visit the market make sure you are early enough, as most of the stands close down around 2:00 pm. The busiest days are Saturday and Sunday.

14. Walk To The Ljubljana Castle, Locals Never Use The Funicular Railway

Ljubljana castle, located proudly over the old city center, is a popular tourist spot. At the same time, it is a popular spot for locals. While tourist enjoy the museums and restaurants located inside the castle, the locals usually just have a walk and relax in the park on the other side of the small hill where the castle is located. The park is not big but offers enjoyable views all around.

You can enter the castle courtyard free of charge and enjoy the view of the city. If you visit on Saturday in the warmer part of the year there is a big chance you will witness a wedding. In the summer the castle becomes alive in the evenings with many concerts, theatre performances, exhibitions and an outdoor cinema.

While most of the tourist use the funicular railway to ascend the hill, none of the locals do so. If you are not too tired from sightseeing or partying the night before I encourage you to walk a short hike from the old city center to the castle. There are many different paths leading to the castle, some steeper than others, but none would be considered hard.

15. Lay Down, Relax And Feed The Squirrels In Park Tivoli

Tivoli is the biggest park in the city. On one side of the park, there is infrastructure for different kinds of sport. The other part is covered with greenery and intersected with many small paths. On the northwest, the paths slowly ascend and if you follow the right path, you can easily end up on Rožnik hill without being aware of it.

On a sunny day, the park is a popular spot for locals to spend the afternoon reading a book, having a picnic, walking a dog or doing some other activities. Nowadays it is also a popular place for group gatherings. In summer, instead indoors, there are all sorts of activities going on in the park like Yoga, Tai Chi, meditation, fencing and dance. In the evenings, the place is a popular dating spot.

In Tivoli park you can relax or explore some of the less visited forest paths in the back of the park. Although Ljubljana, being an extremely safe city, Tivoli is one of the rarest places I would advise you against walking alone at night. If you have to cross it stay on the illuminated paths or do it with a bike.

One thing many people enjoy in the park is feeding the squirrels which are well adapted to people and are not afraid to come closer. Recently the city council decided to make a new law against feeding the wild animals in the city, as there are too many pigeons in the city center. However, the law does not apply to the Tivoli squirrels.

16. Visit Ljubljana ZOO

Although not one of the biggest zoos in Europe, it makes for a nice afternoon trip. Years ago, it used to be in a quite bad condition, later they renovated it and changed it into a lovely place. There is still a lack of educational boards translated into English though.

The zoo is located under Rožnik hill, surrounded by woods. It makes a convenient stop if you are planning to visit Koseški Bajer lake or Rožnik Hill. The lower part of the zoo is more popular. There are more animals, a restaurant, a souvenir shop and a playground. You can see elephants, giraffes, meerkats, different kind of monkeys, bears and many more. The newest inhabitants of the zoo are two lazy cheetahs. The upper part of the zoo is less visited, probably because it is located a short walk up the hill. There you can see ibex, chamois, deer and the stars of the zoo, the lynx.

In the winter of 2014, a big part of Slovenia was handicapped by a strong sleet. Everything froze down and got stuck under a thick layer of ice. Although it looked like a fairy tale, the damage in some parts of the country was very bad. During that time, Ljubljana zoo suffered severe damage. After some of the bigger trees on Rožnik hill broke down due to the weight of the ice, the zoo fences in some parts got torn. This resulted in some animal escapes. One of the lynxes jumped the fence and visited his long-time next-door neighbor, the chamois. The visit did not end up very good for the chamois. The lynx and his female friend run out of the zoo area and enjoyed a week of freedom, wandering around Rožnik hill, in the middle of the city. After a week they hunted down the lady lynx, which was accidentally killed during the action. The male lynx was captured a few days later. Since then the lynx is the star of the zoo, he got named after the hill where he spent his free time; Lynx Rožnik (or Ris Rožnik in Slovene).

17. Have A Morning Jog Around Koseze Pond

The Koseze Pond is a small artificial lake in a former clay pit. It sets a good example of how once an industrial zone was transformed into a reach habitat and a popular area for locals to spend their free time. Around the pond, there is a circular walking path with some benches and lookout piers. The animals living in and around the pond mainly include frogs and numerous other amphibians, several fish species, dragonflies, swans and other bird species.

The Koseze Pond offers an opportunity for fishing for carp, sheatfish, rudd, bass, zander, and several other species. Fishing permits can be purchased from the nearby Gostilna Pri Cvičku restaurant. In summer you can observe several radio-controlled model boat races. If you visit in winter months you can try ice skating. Only try ice skating or walking on the lake if you see other people doing so. If there are no people doing this, the reason is probably the thinness of the ice.

It is a good idea to combine a visit to the pond with a walk on the Path of Remembrance and Comradeship, as the area is located in the immediate vicinity of it.

18. Cycle Your Way Around Ljubljana On POT

The Path of Remembrance and Comradeship is almost 33 km long recreational and memorial circular path around Ljubljana. It is also referred to as "the Trail Along the Wire" or "Ljubljana's green belt". During the World War ll, Fascist Italy annexed the city of Ljubljana. People were subject to repression and after the emergence of resistance, the Italians decided to surround the city with a barbed wire fence to prevent the communication between the city and its surroundings.

The trail is gravel-paved and marked by signposts, information boards and metal markers. One hundred and two octagonal memorial stones were positioned at the exact locations where the bunkers used to stand.

Walking, jogging or cycling the whole or only a part of the path are all very popular with the locals. During snowy winters, cross-country ski tracks are provided at some of the sections. Every year there is a traditional event called "March along the Wire" (Pohod ob Žici) when usually a big crowd gathers to walk the circle around Ljubljana. It happens sometime in the beginning of the May.

Due to Ljubljana's growth over the years, some areas of the path now run through built-up areas. The most noticeable build-up area is the segment from Koseze crossing Klagenfurt Street (Celovška cesta) and Vienna Street (Dunajska cesta), ending near Stožice Stadium.

19. Read A Book On The City "Beach", But Don't Swim!

Ljubljana has its own beach. It's a pity that it's actually not a real beach. The beach is just the way locals call a part of the waterside next to Ljubljanica River. It is located in a part of the city called Trnovo. Trnovski Pristan or Ljubljana beach is easily reachable from the center, just follow the river and walk in the opposite direction of the river flow. It is about 1 km walk from the Triple Bridge.

The beach consists of some concrete steps in the shadow of a few big trees. It is a relaxing place, good for eating a takeaway lunch, reading a book or hanging out with friends. On weekend evenings, it can be packed with drunk teenagers.

Even though it is called a beach, you should not swim here. I am pretty sure it is not allowed anyway. In the past, people could actually swim in the Ljubljanica river. Later they decided the river is not clean enough for swimming. Today, they are considering making an actual beach, where people could really swim in Ljubljanica. I am excited to see how this ends up.

20. Craving Something Sweet?

Slovenians love to treat themselves with sugary sweets. Every occasion is a good enough excuse to sit in a cafe and have a piece of cake beside the usual coffee. In Ljubljana, Kavarna Zvezda and Kavarna Cacao are considered top choice. Beside a piece of cake, you can treat yourself with different kinds of ice coffee, frappes, fruit cups, and other similar desserts. Slovenians are also big ice cream lovers. During summer there are countless ice cream stands around the city. In my opinion, first place in best ice cream award goes to the two cafes listed above. Hint; try a scoop of blueberry taste in Kavarna Cacao. If you are up for pancakes, Romeo restaurant on the shore of River Ljubljanica is a place to go.

There are some traditional Slovenian sweets worth tasting. Most famous are Prekmurska gibanica (layered pastry with a number of fillings that include poppy seeds, cottage cheese, walnuts, apples, and cream), krof (fluffy round fried dough bun filled with delicious apricot jam), apple strudel and kremšnita which you should try while visiting Bled.

"In the small central square of Ljubljana, the statue of the poet stares fixedly at something. If you follow his gaze, you will see, on the other side of the square, the face of a woman carved into the stone of one of the houses. That was where Julia had lived. Even after death, Prešeren gaze for all eternity on his impossible love."

— *Paulo Coelho,*

Veronika Decides to Die

Andreja Dintinjana

21. Take A Walk In The Botanical Garden Of Ljubljana

Ljubljana has its own botanical garden which belongs to The University of Ljubljana's departure of Biology. When built, the garden area was much bigger. Later they shrunk it on a relatively small surface due to the city growth and building of new transportation lines.

The garden contains more than 4.500 different species and subspecies of plants. One-third of them are endemic to Slovenia, while the rest mostly originate from other parts of Europe. It plays an important role in the growing and protection of Slovenia's endemic, endangered, vulnerable and rare species. As a part of the garden, there is a tropical glasshouse which offers you an opportunity to view over 380 plant species native to tropical parts of the world.

If you want to relax in nature after a busy day, but lack the transportation to go out of town, this is a place to go. You can walk around and observe a vast variety of plants, have a drink in a tea house located inside the park or try guessing as many names of the plants as you can. The garden itself has no entrance fee. A small admission fee is charged if you wish to see the glasshouse though. During the night the park is closed.

22. Have A Unique Friday Night Experience On Metelkova – Heart Of Ljubljana's Alternative Culture

Ljubljana is big on alternative culture. Metelkova is like a city on its own within Ljubljana. A complex of former Yugoslav army barracks, taken over by squatters in the nineties, today offers a unique nightlife in town. There are bars and pubs, galleries, concert venues and a hostel. All covered in colorful graffiti and weird art. Most of the nights there is something going on somewhere, but especially on Friday and Saturday nights when you always find a group of friendly people to enjoy the evening with. Here you will find all sorts of people. There are punks, metalheads, hipsters, hippies, LGBT crowd and many different artists. The regular events include everything from a punk and metal concerts to poetry readings and joined cooking sessions with a purpose to share food with the homeless.

People either love or hate Metelkova. If you are just a little bit curious but not sure if you belong in this kind of crowd, you should give it a try. Many tourists visit the place during the day also. If you are not used to this kind of places you might feel threatened by the crowd at first. But the place is generally safe and the people are mostly really friendly, so just give them a chance.

23. Climb Your Way Out Of Foggy Ljubljana

Ljubljana is a very foggy place, especially if you visit anytime from October to March. Due to the closed basin in which the city is located, it is not uncommon for the morning fog to last until 2.00 pm or even the whole day. In the past industry and the coal burning were the reasons for smog in the Ljubljana basin. Nowadays the smog is getting worse due to the traffic and wood used as a fuel in individual homes. It is not Beijing, but there are some days when people are advised not to move around too much, as the amounts of pollutants in the air are too big.

In the foggy part of the year, locals tend to visit the places with a little higher altitude, because above the fog usually, the sky is clear and sunny. Šmarna Gora hill is the most popular place to do so. If you want to blend in with the locals you should put yourself in a line of people trying to climb the hill on a foggy Saturday morning to experience the sunrise. It can really get crowded sometimes. That's why I would advise you to make this trip one foggy morning during the week. If the fog is really thick, the view from up there will be spectacular, something like a pool of clouds beneath you, similar to the view from the airplane.

Of course the hill is nice in the warmer part of the year also. Either you clearly see all of the city, or you see the pool of clouds, the view is always spectacular.

24. Swim In Slovenia's Deepest Lake

Located on the southern edge of Ljubljana Marshes near the village Jezero which can directly be translated into Lake. Not sure if it actually is the deepest lake in Slovenia, as only first 51 meters of it were explored. On the bottom of the lake, there is a chasm, connected with the underground caves nearby. The springs from the area provide the water which then sinks inside the chasm.

The lake is almost totally round and surrounded with hills. There is a nice forest in the area which provides a cooling effect during the hot summer months. During summer it is possible to swim in the lake. It is totally safe, you will not be pulled inside the chasm by some mysterious creatures, although there is a big variety of different sorts of fish in the lake. The lake is also popular with the fisherman who enjoy fishing all year round as the lake rarely freezes.

The spot is a popular starting point for hikers, going to the top of the hills on the southern edge of the Marshes. A cozy lakeside restaurant nearby offers tasty Slovenian food.

25. Enjoy A Coffee With A View

The Ljubljana Skyscraper or Nebotičnik, as we call it, offers amazing views of the city and its surroundings. Don't be surprised if you are having a hard time finding it, as it is only about 70 meters high. You are wondering why somebody would call a 70 meters high building a skyscraper? When it opened it actually was the highest building in Central Europe. Supposedly it was not a very popular building back then, as in people's opinion it was ruining the baroque city image. Nowadays everyone got used to the skyscraper. The building is mostly a combination of residential apartments and some high-profile business offices.

To get to the top use the elevator, although I have seen quite some people enjoying the walk up. On the top of it, there is a cafe from which you can observe the view. The cafe's prices are a bit higher than prices in other places in the city. They usually don't mind if you only come and ask to see the view and take some photos, but wouldn't you prefer to enjoy the view a little bit longer while sipping a coffee?

26. Have A Beer In The Union Brewery

The Union is one of the two bigger Slovenian Beer breweries. It is located very close to the old city center in Ljubljana. The other one is Laško, located in a town of Laško on the eastern side of Slovenia. If you look carefully while walking through the city you will notice most of the people are either drinking one or the other. If you ask a Slovenian about it he or she will tell you one of the two (the one they prefer) is much better and they will never drink the another one. However, nowadays with many small breweries opening up this phenomenon is slowly changing.

The Union pub is a very popular place to enjoy a good dinner and try out different types of Union beer. Book ahead, as it can get crowded, especially during the weekends. They are also offering a "Union experience" where you are able to visit some parts of the brewery and get familiar with the process of beer making.

27. Listen To A Summer Concert In Križanke

Križanke is an open-air theater set up inside the former 18th-century Monastery of the Holy Cross. It is one of the works of the architect Jože Plečnik. Today it is mostly used for different summer festivals, set in the main open-air stage or in other venues; Križanke Church, the Knight's Hall or the Courtyard of Hell. The southern courtyard with its large retractable canopy has proven to be the perfect location for concerts with its amphitheater-like shape.

If you have a chance to be part of an event happening in Križanke, you should not miss it. One part of the complex is open to the public and you can have a look at it even if there is no event happening that day. If you are an architecture enthusiast or if you appreciated other works of Jože Plečnik, you should definitely visit it.

28. Looking For A Swimming Pool?

Swimming pool Kolezija, built in 1853, is the oldest swimming pool in Ljubljana. Around that time, Ljubljana was considered to be the place with the best swimming pools in the area. Later the pool was abandoned and luckily renovated again a few years ago. Today, during the summer months, it is open for public and it got quite popular as it is the only swimming pool near Ljubljana center where you can enjoy swimming even in the evening, up until 10:00 pm.

The biggest complex of swimming pools in Ljubljana is Atlantis Water Park, located next to the shopping malls of BTC. They like to praise about having 16 swimming pools (two outdoors) and 15 saunas. On a rainy day, if you don't have the opportunity to take a one-day trip into one of the Thermal Spas, this might be a good option.

29. Try Traditional Balkan Food

Enjoy the fact that you are visiting one of the Balkan countries while tasting some traditional Balkan food. Even if some people try to convince you Slovenia is not a Balkan country, I tell you the opposite. It is true that our culture is, in many ways, much different than for example Bosnian or Serbian culture. However, we were a part of Yugoslavia and that means we still belong to this group of countries.

There are plenty of traditional Balkan restaurants in Ljubljana. Some of the most known are Gostilna Pri Čadu, Sarajevo 84 and Das Ist Valter. I recommend you take a few hours of rest after the meal, as this is not the light type of food.

Slovenians love a taste of grilled minced meat called čevapčiči (pronounced "chevapchichi"). It is considered a typical barbeque food. You must know though, that this is not a traditional Slovenian food.

30. SUP Your Way Through The City

Ljubljana is supposedly the only European capital where you have a chance to stand-up paddle-board through the heart of the city. Paddling on the River Ljubljanica gives you a chance to see the city from the unique perspective. The meeting point for the SUP activity is at the café Špica, about 10 minutes walking distance from the Prešeren Square.

Don't get scared if you see a coypu (also called nutria), a big rat-like animal, wandering around the river and its shore. Originally South-American rodent were brought in the city in the past with the intention of breeding them for fur. Today, due to the lack of predators, they are widespread around the River Ljubljanica. They are not dangerous but do not test your luck by trying to pet them either.

Andreja Dintinjana

"As you travel around Slovenia,

Think of the tales the hills could tell you.

Share the awe of natural wonder;

Tread the trails, but as you wander

Honor the age-old endeavors to be

Literate, informed, democratic and free."

— Jacqueline Widmar Stewart

Andreja Dintinjana

31. Cool Down On A Hot Summer Day In Iška Gorge

On the edge of Ljubljana Marshes there is Iški Vintgar, a scenic gorge of the Iška River. A walk through the gorge offers an opportunity to see the river and the surrounding scenery with its numerous sandbanks, river pools and steep rocky banks. The place is popular in hot summer months as the river is relatively cold and offers a nice cooling place. Real swimming is possible only in some parts of the river, where the water is deep enough. With the gorge, providing a lot of shadow, the place can be relatively dark. Consider this if you are visiting in winter months and go in the middle of the day when the sun is at its highest.

This is also a very popular picnic location. You can rent a picnic place with a place to grill for €3 per person. Some are next to the river where you get your own small river beach. About one hour walk from Iški Vintgar there is a World War II partisan hospital well worth visiting. From the hospital, several waymarked paths lead to the nearby hills of Rakitna, Krim and Bloke.

32. Have A Walk Through The Village In The Middle Of Ljubljana

If you walk through the neighborhood of Krakovo you feel like you are walking through the village. You can observe the old houses from stone, built like the ones in Slovenian countryside, vegetable gardens and dogs, each one guarding their owner's property. To the first time visitor, it may seem just like a Slovenian village. It is easy to forget you are actually located in the center of Ljubljana.

I the past, the neighborhood used to be a village where people were mostly farmers and fisherman. Every day they supplied the city with fresh food. While city grew bigger, Krakovo slowly became one of its neighborhoods. There is not much to do there, but it is relatively close to many other sights and it is an interesting place to see indeed.

33. Visit The Famous Cemetery

Žale cemetery, the biggest Slovenian cemetery, is located in Bežigrad district in Ljubljana. It is 'home' to a number of Slovenian actors, writers, painters and the architect Jože Plečnik, among whose many famous creations is also this cemetery. The cemetery is best known for its ornamental gates and chapels. With 375.000 square meters, it serves more as a park today. If you are not creeped out by the graves consider taking a walk in the area.

Avoid this area around the first week of November as All Saints' Day, the national holiday is happening in Slovenia. Around this week all the families visit the graveyards. As a result, almost every year there is a traffic collapse around Žale cemetery. On the other hand, it might be interesting to see the amount of candles and flowers laid on the graves and in front of the cemetery during the holiday.

34. Explore The Village Of Bistra

Bistra is a village, located on the southwestern part of Ljubljana Marshes. It is known for the old and impressive monastery, which was built across the main road. On one side of the monastery building, there is a spring with water so clear you barely notice it's there. Be careful while walking on the road as from the time the monastery was built a few centuries ago, there was considerable growth in traffic. Once a broad road under the building today represents the main obstacle where the vehicles have to wait on either one side or the other.

On the other side of the spring, there is a renovated Technical museum with a nice garden around the spring and a forest nature trail. Nearby there is a restaurant where Slovenian cuisine is offered.

35. Try The Traditional Slovenian Cuisine

Slovenian cuisine comes in numerous tastes and shapes. The influence of diverse Slovenian landscapes, climate, history and neighboring cultures each shaped the cuisine in its own way. Literally, every region has its own selection of traditional foods.

Saturday lunch is, in most families, still considered the most important meal of the week when the whole family gathers, traditionally sometime between noon and one o'clock, to enjoy the lunch together. The Sunday lunch usually begins with Beef soup, followed by mashed potatoes, stake in some sauce and lattice as a side dish.

Traditional main dishes you have to try are; goulash (pieces of meat stewed on a slow fire for a long time), jota (soup with sauerkraut or sour turnip, kidney beans and potatoes), štruklji (rolled dumplings with sweet or sour filling), Kraški Pršut (ham from a thigh of pork, rubbed with salt), njoki (potato dumplings), mushroom soup and traditional Carniolan sausages.

There are many restaurants in the old part of Ljubljana, offering traditional Slovenian cuisine. You can try at Slovenska Hiša (The Slovenian House) or in Vodnikov Hram. If you don't feel like sitting down for lunch, you can stop at Klobasarna and order a takeaway Carniolan sausage.

36. When The Locals Dine Out

The locals in Ljubljana don't usually eat at the traditional Slovenian restaurants, as their mothers and grandmothers make this kind of food on Sundays. There is a variety of restaurants serving all sorts of food in Ljubljana, however, locals mostly go for a pizza. A typical get-together night with friends would start with a pizza at one of many amazing pizza places in town, followed by a beer or two (or three) in a pub of choice.

You will notice that Italian food is very popular with the Slovenians. We kind of stole some dishes, redesigned them and made them our own. A good example is pasta with "Slovenian" type of sauce or risotto, made with local ingredients.
The best pizza places in town are Foculus, Parma or Pizzeria Trta.

37. Friday Lunch At Open Kitchen

Open Kitchen (Odprta Kuhna) is a weekly food market and it is the place to be every Friday. There are over 50 stands, each one representing one of the restaurants in the city or around. There is a broad choice of international as well as local cuisine. The portions are not big as it is considered more like a tryout, but the prices are friendly and nobody is stopping you from ordering at more different stands and eating until you are full.

The main event is happening at Ljubljana's Central Market. If the Friday is warm and sunny, be prepared for the crowd.

38. Coffee Culture

You will rarely find a place with so many cafes, full with the locals, as there are in Ljubljana. What can we say, we are a coffee culture. And in Slovenia, the coffee is good, really good. We prepare coffee in two main ways. Either we drink the Italian type of coffee made with an espresso machine or Turkish coffee made with džezva – Turkish coffee pot, which we inherited from our Bosnian friends.

The Slovenian way of drinking coffee is slow and mostly includes talking. It is more of a gathering with a friend, the coffee may be just an excuse. It came that far, that we rarely call a friend and invite them for a chat or for a walk, we usually invite them for a coffee. It does not really matter if then we drink tea instead or don't even sit down in a cafe for that matter. So if somebody invites you for a coffee don't look too surprised if it never comes to that, you might just get offered a beer instead.

Andreja Dintinjana

If you wish to do it Slovenian way, sit in a cafe with a friend any time during the day, as there is no time limit for ordering a coffee, and take your time for about one-hour long chat. If you and your friend steel feel like talking, just move to the bar next door and order a beer. Any time after 12.00 drinking beer is socially excepted.

39. Try To Find Something Useful On The Flea Market

Don't be surprised if you see a bunch of people loafing around the shore of Ljubljanica Sunday morning, it's a flea market time. Along riverside Breg south of Cobblers' Bridge every Sunday a few stands appear where you can find random knickknacks, vintage postcards and other quirky memorabilia. It usually looks like a place Ljubljana unloads its junk.

Don't expect too much, but there are always treasures to find along the trash. Especially if you are some sort of a collector or a communist enthusiast.

40. Take A One Day Trip

Slovenia is a small country and Ljubljana is located right in the middle of it. You can hardly find a place in Slovenia where from Ljubljana you would not be able to arrive within 3 hours of driving. This, combined with the fact that Slovenia has so many incredible places to visit, are the main reasons every tourist who spends more than one day in Ljubljana takes at least one trip to explore some other part of the country too. Even though Ljubljana has a lot to offer, you just cannot miss an opportunity to do the same. If you are more of an independent traveler, your best option is to rent a car and try to explore the places on your own with the help of a good navigation system. There are numerous agencies you can find online or scattered around the city center, that are able to arrange a trip for you. Try asking in the tourist information center.

On the next few pages, I will present you some ideas for a one-day trip you can take from Ljubljana.

>TOURIST

"Travel brings power and love back into your life."

— *Rumi*

Andreja Dintinjana

41. Visit A Cave

Postojna cave, far the most popular cave in the country, is often crowded with tourists. You will find it approximately 40 minutes west from Ljubljana if you take the highway. There is a tourist train that takes you inside where you walk in line and observe spectacular stalagmites, stalactites and other cave features. If you don't mind the crowd it is one of the most fascinating sights in this part of Europe. If you decide to visit you should not miss Predjama Castle, a Renaissance castle built within a caves' mouth, located some 9 kilometers away from Postojna Cave.

Not the most famous caves in Slovenia, however the nicest ones if you ask me, are the Škocjan Caves, located a little bit further down the same highway. With far less daily visits the experience they offer is much more unique. The caves are a part of UNESCO natural and cultural world heritage sites and are protected under Ramsar convention as an underground wetland. Although the stalactites and stalagmites are not as big as in Postojna Cave, you will be fascinated by the enormous river canyon located inside a big cave hall. In the Park of Škocjan Caves, there are many more features worth seeing. Some of them are two big collapsed dolines, a chasm and a gorge of River Reka, which has an interesting name as it can be translated into River, so it is basically called the River River.

If you are looking for a really unique caving experience, there are a vast amount of other caves you can explore in Slovenia. Your best option is to ask at the tourist office, they can advise you one that will fit your time, physical shape and group size criteria.

42. Bled Or Bohinj?

Probably the first photo of Slovenia you saw was the one from Bled, showing the beautiful island on the lake with the church on it. It really is amazingly beautiful there all year round. The fact that this is by far the most touristic place in Slovenia is not surprising at all. Therefore, especially in high season, there are too many visitors around the lake, which makes it hard to really enjoy the nature and the beauty of Bled.

This is the reason many locals prefer the neighboring Lake Bohinj. Lake Bohinj is the biggest permanent natural lake in Slovenia. It lays in a peaceful environment surrounded by mountains and it is a popular starting point for many hikes. Popular activities on and around the lake also include swimming, cycling, fishing, rock climbing, paragliding and sailing. There is a continuous problem with the parking so inquire about your options before you go on this trip if you are traveling by car.

Andreja Dintinjana

If you are in the neighborhood, you should definitely not miss Savica Waterfall and Mostnica Gorge or even more spectacular Vintgar Gorge in Bled.

43. Hiking

Slovenians are very passionate about hiking, you don't need to be a scientist to realize that. A typical Slovene would spend most of their sunny weekends in the mountains.

Inside the city of Ljubljana and in the close vicinity, there are a few hills that locals mostly visit as a quick afternoon walk or a morning exercise. Right in the center of Ljubljana there is Castle Hill. Close to it there is Rožnik Hill on one side and a little bit bigger Golovec Hill, on the other side. In close vicinity, the most popular are Šmarna Gora Hill or Rašica, both north of Ljubljana. South of Ljubljana Marshes there are a lot of hills to choose from too.

If you wish to do a more serious hike, you should travel a little bit further out of Ljubljana. Your best option is to head north, for the Alps, although in almost all the country's regions you can find a hill to walk to. There are as many options for a good hike in

Slovenia as there are different kinds of people. Everything depends on your desires and physical abilities.

It is important to point out the importance of the appropriate hiking equipment. Every year there are at least few cases of deaths or injuries due to the inappropriate equipment or overrated physical abilities. Make sure to always wear appropriate hiking shoes and have warm clothes. Even during the summer, the temperatures in the mountains can fall below zero.

44. To The Coast

If you wish to visit sunnier, Mediterranean part of the country, you should head west, for the coast. One hour drive from often foggy Ljubljana, many times you can enjoy totally different weather conditions.

It is not a surprise that the city of Piran, with its narrow streets and compact houses, is one of main tourist attractions. Because it was built under the Venetian influence, the same as other two main coastal towns of Koper and Izola, the difference with other Slovenian towns in the city architecture and street layout is obvious. In Piran, you should not miss a relatively steep but totally worth climb to the city walls where you can observe the amazing view of the city. There are big saltpans close to Piran also worth taking a look if you are in the neighborhood.

The city of Koper is the biggest settlement on the coast. It is known by the only port of Slovenia. Izola in many ways still looks like a traditional fishing town as it used to be. There are breathtaking cliffs in Strunjan and typical Istrian villages in the outskirts. While there you should treat yourself with some fresh seafood and a glass of local wine.

45. Go Wine Tasting

Wine has a crucial importance in Slovenian culture. Even our national anthem in one part talks about wine. There are 22.300 hectares of vineyards in the country, annually making around 85 million liters of wine, almost all of it is consumed domestically. This is not bad if you have in mind that Slovenia only has around 2 million inhabitants. There are three principal wine regions; the Drava Wine-growing Region, the Lower Sava Wine-growing Region and the Littoral Wine-growing Region. Observing the landscape, you notice many vineyards are located along slopes or hillsides in terraced rows. In the steep terrains, the harvesting is still done manually. Although you can do wine tasting in Ljubljana, much better option is to combine it with a one-day trip into one of the wine regions where you can visit some wineries and see the process of winemaking. The most interesting for a visit are Brda, Kras, Radgona, Jeruzalem and Haloze.

46. Soča Adrenaline Sports

Slovenians are big fans of adrenaline sports. The most popular are the ones happening in, on or next to the river, which is not surprising as there are so many rivers in the area. For lovers of wild and fast rapids, the River Soča is the best choice. You can try rafting, kayaking, and hydrospeeding. Every year more popular canyoning enables visitors to experience picturesque gorges, waterfalls and pools.

The scenery in the Soča Valley is worth seeing even if the adrenaline sports are not your thing. The water is famous for its unique turquoise color, which makes a nice contrast with the vast forests and mountains in the background. Be careful though, if you manage to fall into the water, even in the middle of the summer, the freezing cold might shock you. There are good options for budgie jumping from one of the bridges in the area also.

From Ljubljana head to the west. There is about 2 hour drive to the valley, depends which part of it you decide to reach.

47. Have A Relaxing Day In The Spa

One of the best features in Slovenia are its many thermal and mineral springs located on the eastern part of the country. Many are reachable from the capital within an hour or two.

Terme Čatež are the largest ones with a big complex of pools located indoors as well as outdoors. This is your best choice if traveling with small children. Others include Wellness Centre of Dolenjske Toplice, Thermana Laško, Terme Dobrna spa, Terme Olimia spa, Thermana Laško and a little bit further away Moravske Toplice and Terme Lendava spa. The choice is up to you and depends on your time, transportation options and budget.

If spending the whole day in a spa is too much for you, a good idea is to enjoy half of the day in Terme Ptuj and spend other half exploring the oldest city in Slovenia, the picturesque Ptuj.

Spas can be a wonderful choice in the winter, when after a few busy days exploring you can finally totally heat up your body in the warm spring waters. Even better if it is snowing outside, as there is no better feeling than swimming in the hot pool outdoors while snowflakes are falling on your face.

48. Bear Safari

Are you looking for an experience you will never forget? Try bear watching. Recently tourist agencies in Slovenia started offering this really unique experience. It is actually a great idea, as there are a lot of brown bears in Slovenian woods, particularly in the southern part of the country.

The idea is that, accompanied with an experienced guide, you go deep into the forest where you climb on the treetop hunting lookout. If you are lucky you can see one or more bears or a female bear with cubs, as well as other wild animals. Of course, nobody can guarantee you will actually see the bear.

49. Visit The Big Pasture Plateau

Velika Planina is a mountain plateau with the average elevation of 1.500 meters above sea level. It is located about 50 kilometers north from Ljubljana. The plateau is well known for its green pastures and numerous herdsmen's settlements.

Spend your day wandering around the green pastures of the plateau, treat yourself with the famous dish Štruklji in the mountain cabin and admire the unique architecture of the cottages. In some of them you can taste and buy locally produced dairy goods.

For those, who are more active, the mountain offers ideal possibilities for hiking and various mountain-cycling tours. During the winter, a small ski resort is attracting the guests. If you are lucky and manage to visit the plateau in spring, just in time when the snow didn't totally melt down yet and the flowers just started to blossom, you might be able to see the astonishing flower carpet with millions of flowers underneath your feet.

If you don't feel like hiking, you can ascend the plateau with a cable car starting a few kilometers northeast from the town of Kamnik.

50. Souvenir Ideas

There are countless souvenir shops in the old part of Ljubljana, mostly selling the same types of souvenirs. The biggest one is located on the edge of the city market, next to the statue of Valentin Vodnik.

If you want to bring home something useful and yet typical, good options are some of the locally made jams, honey, salt from the saltpans of Sečovlje, olive oil or pumpkin seed oil, special chocolate, herbal tea, a piece of traditional cheese or a piece of Kraški Pršut. If you want to treat your friends at home with the taste of Slovenian alcohol, a good choice is any wine or locally produced liqueurs like Borovničke (blubbery liqueur), Brinjevec (Juniper liqueur), Orehovec (Nut liqueur), Viljamovka (Pear liqueur) or Slivovka (Plum liqueur).

Top Reasons to Book This Trip

- **Nature**: Ljubljana is one of the greenest European capitals. Situated in the center of Slovenia, you are always only a step away from every nature lover's dreams.
- **Food**: We took a little bit from everyone and made an unique mix with it.
- **Culture**: Experience Berlin, Prague and Rome all in one. Ljubljana is small in size, yet it will amaze you with its rich cultural mix.

Andreja Dintinjana

> TOURIST

GREATER THAN A TOURIST

Visit GreaterThanATourist.com
http://GreaterThanATourist.com

Sign up for the Greater Than a Tourist Newsletter
http://eepurl.com/cxspyf

Follow us on Facebook:
https://www.facebook.com/GreaterThanATourist

Follow us on Pinterest:
http://pinterest.com/GreaterThanATourist

Follow us on Instagram:
http://Instagram.com/GreaterThanATourist

Andreja Dintinjana

> TOURIST

GREATER THAN A TOURIST

Please leave your honest review of this book on Amazon and Goodreads. Thank you.

We appreciate your positive and negative feedback as we try to provide tourist guidance in their next trip from a local.

Our Story

Traveling is a passion of the "Greater than a Tourist" series creator. Lisa studied abroad in college, and for their honeymoon Lisa and her husband toured Europe. During her travels to Malta, an older man tried to give her some advice based on his own experience living on the island since he was a young boy. She was not sure if she should talk to the stranger but was interested in his advice. When traveling to some places she was wary to talk to locals because she was afraid that they weren't being genuine. Through her travels, Lisa learned how much locals had to share with tourists. Lisa created the "Greater Than a Tourist" book series to help connect people with locals. A topic that locals are very passionate about sharing.

Andreja Dintinjana

Notes

Printed in Great Britain
by Amazon